# GREAT MOMENTS IN
# *Baseball*

*by Michael Burgan*

**WORLD ALMANAC® LIBRARY**

Please visit our web site at: www.worldalmanaclibrary.com
For a free color catalog describing World Almanac® Library's
list of high-quality books and multimedia programs,
call 1-800-848-2928 (USA) or 1-800-387-3178 (Canada).
World Almanac® Library's fax: (414) 332-3567.

**Library of Congress Cataloging-in-Publication Data**

Burgan, Michael.
    Great moments in baseball / by Michael Burgan. —— North American ed.
      p. cm. —— (Great moments in sports)
    Summary: Recounts ten high points in the history of baseball, including Ted Williams' 1941 season,
Jackie Robinson becoming the first African American major league player, and Nolan Ryan's seventh
no-hitter.
    Includes bibliographical references and index.
    ISBN 0-8368-5344-X (lib. bdg.)
    ISBN 0-8368-5358-X (softcover)
    1. Baseball—United States—History—Juvenile literature. [1. Baseball—History.] I. Title.
II. Great moments in sports (Milwaukee, Wis.)
    GV867.5.B87   2002
    796.357'0973—dc21                   2002016865

This North American edition first published in 2002 by
**World Almanac® Library**
330 West Olive Street, Suite 100
Milwaukee, WI 53212 USA

This U.S. edition © 2002 by World Almanac® Library.

An Editorial Directions book
Editor: Lucia Raatma
Photo researcher: Image Select International Ltd.
Copy editor: Melissa McDaniel
Proofreader: Sarah De Capua
Indexer: Tim Griffin
Art direction, design, and page production: The Design Lab
World Almanac® Library editorial direction: Mark J. Sachner
World Almanac® Library art direction: Tammy Gruenewald
World Almanac® Library production: Susan Ashley and Jessica L. Yanke

Photographs ©: Getty Images, cover, 3, 5, 6; Corbis, 7, 8; Getty Images, 9, 10, 11; Corbis,
12, 13; Getty Images, 14; Corbis, 15 top; Getty Images, 15 bottom, 17, 18, 19, 20; Corbis,
21, 22, 23, 24, 25, 26, 27, 28, 29, 30; Getty Images, 31; Corbis, 32, 33; Getty Images, 34,
35, 36, 37; Corbis, 38 top; Getty Images, 38 bottom, 39, 41; Corbis, 42; Getty Images, 43;
AFP, 44; Getty Images, 45; Getty Images, 46 top, bottom left; Corbis, 46 top right; Getty
Images, 46 bottom right.

Printed in the United States of America

1 2 3 4 5 6 7 8 9 06 05 04 03 02

Opposite: *By the time Cal Ripken Jr. had played his
record-setting 2,632nd consecutive game, he had
established himself as a major league class act.*

# Contents

# Introduction

From the mound, the pitcher throws a high, hard one. The batter, eager at the plate, swings—and connects. As the ball flies off the bat, fielders move into position, runners sprint from their bases, and fans jump from their seats, caught up in the excitement of another baseball game.

Baseball has been called America's national pastime. Children play it in backyards, and millions of people cheer on their favorite major league teams. Americans have enjoyed playing and watching a game similar to and sometimes called baseball since at least the 1770s, though the early game was much different from what is played today. Teams then might have had as many as twenty-five players on the field, and fielders could make an out by hitting runners with a thrown ball.

The modern rules of baseball began taking shape in the 1840s, with nine players in the field,

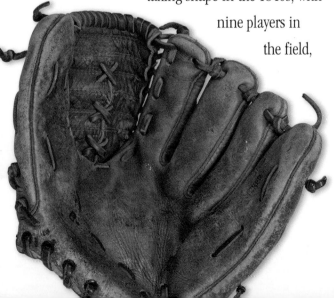

three outs to a side, and no more beaning runners with the ball. After the Civil War, baseball became a national sport, and the first professional team, the Cincinnati Red Stockings, emerged in 1869. Leagues of pro teams developed soon after. The National League of Professional Baseball Clubs formed in 1876, marking the beginning of what is now known as the major leagues. The American League followed in 1901. With both leagues in existence, that year marks the start of modern professional baseball.

The World Series, the championship series between the best teams in the American and National Leagues, began in 1903. The "Fall Classic" is the oldest championship in U.S. professional team sports, and it has produced some of baseball's most memorable games. In 1933, baseball also had the first All-Star game in U.S. professional sports, bringing together the best players from both leagues.

Today, America's national pastime is an international game. The major leagues have teams in Canada, and players from Asia, Australia, and Latin America share the field with North Americans. Professional baseball also reaches into hundreds of smaller cities and towns across North America, as the minor leagues help develop tomorrow's stars.

*Yankee Stadium in October 1996 during the World Series matchup between the New York Yankees and the Atlanta Braves.*

Baseball is also big business. Many players earn millions of dollars a year, and owners pay hundreds of millions of dollars to buy teams. Sometimes it seems the money involved is more important than baseball itself. Most fans, though, still cherish the competition and rooting for the home team. And players still welcome the chance to hit the game-winning home run, strike out a batter, or make a diving catch— some of the great moments of baseball.

With such a long history, baseball has had many extraordinary players and great moments.

Some of these moments have happened in a single game; others have stretched out over a season or capped a career. Choosing only ten for this book was difficult. Some achievements are so great, no one would argue whether they should be included. Other great moments, however, are not so clear-cut. For fans and players alike, recounting and debating such moments are part of the pleasure of the game. Baseball's historic high points could fill several books like this one. Here is one view of ten great moments in baseball.

# THE LONGEST STREAK

## Joe DiMaggio Hits in Fifty-six Consecutive Games

On May 15, 1941, Joe DiMaggio stepped to the plate to face Eddie Smith of the Chicago White Sox. The "Yankee Clipper" reached base with a single, his only hit of the game. That single started the longest hitting streak ever in major league baseball, and it helped guarantee DiMaggio's place in the Hall of Fame.

DiMaggio, center fielder for the New York Yankees, was already a star. The American League's Most Valuable Player in 1939, he had helped the Yankees win four World Series since 1936. DiMaggio smashed home runs and hit for a high average, and his

*In 1941, Joe DiMaggio set a standard of baseball excellence by hitting safely in fifty-six consecutive games.*

fielding was almost flawless. He also knew something about hitting streaks—in 1933, during his first full season in the minor leagues, he had hit in sixty-one consecutive games.

### Start of a Streak

DiMaggio's hit on May 15 came in a losing cause—the fifth Yankee loss in a row. The next day, DiMaggio hit a home run and a triple to help New York beat the Chicago White Sox. As May went on, the Yankees won a few more games, and DiMaggio kept hitting. Some days he managed just a single. Other times, he hit long home

*Joe DiMaggio hitting in his forty-second consecutive game, which broke Sisler's mark.*

runs. By the end of the month, DiMaggio's streak had reached sixteen games, and fans and sports writers began to notice.

In June, DiMaggio had a few close calls when his streak almost ended. Playing the White Sox again, DiMaggio hit a hard grounder to the third baseman, who couldn't make the play. The official scorer ruled it a hit, not an error on the fielder, and the streak reached twenty-five games.

Later in the month, against the St. Louis Browns, it took a double in DiMaggio's last at bat to keep the streak alive at thirty-eight.

By then, DiMaggio was closing in on the official major league record, held by George Sisler, of hitting in forty-one consecutive games. Everyone in baseball knew how close "Joltin' Joe" was to the record (though he said he didn't really start paying attention until he reached

*DiMaggio scoring on July 16, 1941, his fifty-sixth consecutive game with a hit.*

thirty-three games). Many pitchers weren't eager to help DiMaggio. Some tried to throw the ball away from the plate, preferring to walk him rather than give him something good to hit. DiMaggio faced one of those pitchers in game forty. Johnny Babich of the Philadelphia A's threw three pitches far off the plate. "The next pitch was outside too," DiMaggio later said, "but I caught it good and lined it right past Babich."

## BY THE NUMBERS

*Joe DiMaggio's offensive numbers during his hitting streak*

| G | AB | Hits | 2B | 3B | HR | RBI | Runs | BB | Avg |
|----|-----|------|----|----|----|-----|------|----|------|
| 56 | 223 | 91 | 16 | 4 | 15 | 55 | 56 | 21 | .408 |

## A New Record—and More

DiMaggio broke Sisler's record on June 29, during the second game of a doubleheader against the Washington Senators. The hit came on his fourth and last at bat of the game, and the fans cheered him for five minutes. Next up for DiMaggio was the old record of forty-four games, set by "Wee" Willie Keeler in 1897. Although Keeler's streak was not recognized by major league officials, it still meant something to DiMaggio. He passed that mark on July 2 with a home run against the Boston Red Sox. Now everyone wondered how long DiMaggio could go on. The streak reached fifty games on July 11, as DiMaggio belted four hits against the St. Louis Browns. A few days later, DiMaggio had three hits against the Cleveland Indians—his fifty-sixth consecutive game with a hit. Finally, on July 17, DiMaggio went 0 for 3, ending the streak. After the game, DiMaggio said, "I can't say that I'm glad it's over." Years later he added, "I wanted it to go on forever."

The Yanks won forty-one of the fifty-six games during DiMaggio's streak, propelling them into first place in the American League. New York went on to win the World Series, beating the Brooklyn Dodgers in five games. DiMaggio once again won the league MVP award, having set a record that no other player has come close to topping in more than sixty years.

*Above: A Yankee program and scorecard from the 1951 season, Joltin' Joe's last year in the majors.*

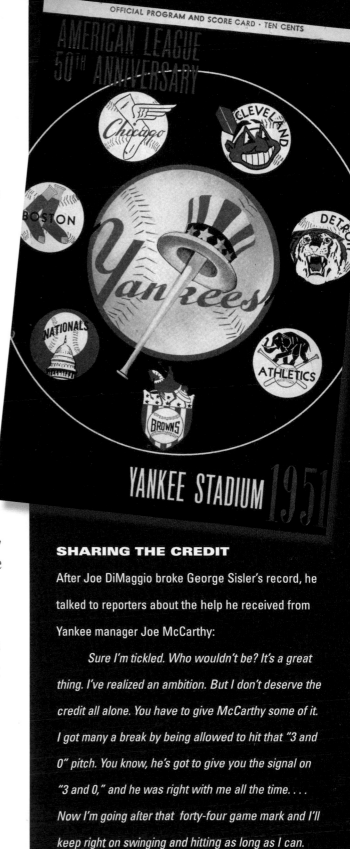

### SHARING THE CREDIT

After Joe DiMaggio broke George Sisler's record, he talked to reporters about the help he received from Yankee manager Joe McCarthy:

*Sure I'm tickled. Who wouldn't be? It's a great thing. I've realized an ambition. But I don't deserve the credit all alone. You have to give McCarthy some of it. I got many a break by being allowed to hit that "3 and 0" pitch. You know, he's got to give you the signal on "3 and 0," and he was right with me all the time. . . . Now I'm going after that forty-four game mark and I'll keep right on swinging and hitting as long as I can.*

# HIGH MARKS FOR THE KID

## Ted Williams Hits .406 for the 1941 Season

Some sportswriters like to point out that a baseball player has the only job in which you can fail seven times out of ten and still be a star. Hitting .300 for a season marks a solid hitter. Bat .300 for a career and a player is on his way to the Hall of Fame in Cooperstown, New York.

In baseball history, only a handful of pros ever hit .400 for a season. Since 1930, only one player has done it—Ted Williams of the Boston Red Sox. In 1941, the same year Joe DiMaggio hit in fifty-six consecutive games, Williams entertained baseball fans with his effort to reach .400.

*Baseball great Ted Williams—cool, confident, and capable both on and off the field.*

At the time, Williams was known as "the Kid," a brash young player who entered the majors in 1939. He hit .327 and .344 his first two seasons, and he promised even more at the start of 1941. "I ask you, how can they stop me from hitting?" Williams said to reporters. "They can't, that's all." Along with his self-confidence, Williams had tremendous vision, which helped him pick up the ball as soon as it left a pitcher's hand. He also studied batting as if it were a science, and his skills helped him become perhaps the greatest hitter in baseball history.

## Slow Start

Williams began the 1941 season with a broken ankle that kept him out of the starting lineup. As a pinch hitter in the Red Sox's first game, he rapped a single, then left for a pinch runner. A week later, he made his first start and went 2 for 4. On May 15, Williams was hitting .336 and he started a twenty-three-game hitting streak—the same day DiMaggio started his historic streak.

When Joe DiMaggio's streak finally ended on July 17, most baseball fans turned their attention to Williams and his quest for .400. He also earned the spotlight earlier in July at the All-Star game, where his three-run homer in the bottom of the ninth gave the American League a 7–5 victory. "That's the best hit I ever made," Williams later said.

*Williams hit an incredible .406 in 1941.*

## BY THE NUMBERS

*Ted Williams's major hitting statistics for 1941*

| G | AB | H | 2B | 3B | HR | RBI | R | BB | AVG |
|---|----|----|-----|-----|-----|------|-----|-----|------|
| 143 | 456 | 185 | 33 | 3 | 37 | 120 | 135 | 145 | .406 |

*Williams being congratulated for his three-run homer in the ninth inning of the 1941 All-Star game.*

Near the end of July, Williams's average fell a bit, but he quickly raised it back up. A month later, he was batting .414, and his hits included some tremendous home runs. Williams struggled at times to keep his average up, because many opposing pitchers preferred to walk him rather than give him good pitches to hit. Williams also felt the pressure of reporters and fans every time he went to the plate.

## Dramatic Finish

By the end of September, with just two games to play, Williams was hitting .39955—technically, .400. Red Sox manager Joe Cronin suggested Williams sit out the season-ending doubleheader against the Philadelphia A's. The Kid refused. "If I couldn't hit .400 all the way," Williams later wrote, "I didn't deserve it."

In his first at bat, Williams grounded a

single past the first baseman. The next time up, he hit a blast out of the ballpark for his thirty-seventh home run—tops in the American League. He finished the game four-for-five, then capped the season with a two-for-three perform-ance in the second game. His final batting aver-age was .406.

Since 1941, only a few players have come close to hitting .400. Tony Gwynn of the San Diego Padres hit .394 in 1994, but that season was cut short by a baseball players' strike. Williams himself hit .388 in 1957, when he was thirty-nine years old. Just five more hits during that season, and Williams would have reached .400 again. After miss-ing almost five seasons during the prime of his career due to military service, he finished his career with a .344 life-time average. Many sports fans wonder what kind of total numbers the Hall of Famer might have had if he had played those years.

*A familiar sight in base-ball parks throughout the American League in 1941—Ted Williams swinging and putting the ball in play.*

## A STUDENT OF THE GAME

In his autobiography, *My Turn at Bat*, Ted Williams described what it took to become a great hitter:

*I think, surely, to hit .400 you have to be an outstanding hitter having everything go just right, and in my case the hitter was a guy who lived to hit. . . . Choose any of the noted hitters, and none of them hit any more balls, swung a bat in practice any more times than Theodore Samuel Williams . . . in order to do the toughest thing there is to do in sport—hit a baseball properly—a man has got to devote every ounce of his concentration to it. . . . I was a guy who practiced until the blisters bled, and then practiced some more.*

# THE BARRIER COMES DOWN

## Jackie Robinson Becomes the First African-American to Play Major League Baseball

*Jackie Robinson, shown here playing for the Brooklyn Dodgers, was admired for both his superior hitting and his outstanding fielding.*

In 1947, the United States was segregated. In many places, particularly in the South, segregation was the law of the land. African-Americans and whites did not go to the same schools, eat in the same restaurants, or stay in the same hotels. In professional baseball, they also did not play on the same fields—until Jackie Robinson broke the color barrier, the unwritten rule that had kept blacks out of the major leagues.

Robinson was a gifted athlete in almost every sport. He was also a proud man who refused to accept the laws and attitudes that denied blacks equal rights. During World War II (1939–1945), Robinson served in the U.S. Army and reached the rank of lieutenant. One day, on a bus in Texas, the driver ordered him to sit in the rear—in the seats reserved for blacks. Robinson refused and was arrested. Robinson won his military trial and proved his determination to confront segregation.

Another man played a key role in breaking baseball's color barrier—Branch Rickey, general manager of the Brooklyn Dodgers. Rickey knew many talented black athletes played baseball in the Negro Leagues. These professional leagues for blacks produced such stars as Josh Gibson, Buck Leonard, and Cool Papa Bell. All of them were big-league material, but because they were black, none ever made it to the majors. By 1945, Rickey was ready to have a Negro League player on the Dodgers—whether the other teams, or the country, were ready or not.

*Before Robinson broke the color barrier, African-American players were allowed to play only in the Negro Leagues. Shown here are (left to right) Art Pennington, Herman Andrews, and Alex Radcliffe of the Chicago Giants.*

*Branch Rickey, general manager of the Brooklyn Dodgers, knew that integration was long overdue in major league baseball, and he boldly encouraged Robinson to break the color barrier.*

## Battling Racism in the Ballpark

Rickey knew it would take a special person to withstand the abuse of racist fans and players. When Robinson first met Rickey, he asked, "Do you want a ballplayer who is afraid to fight back?" Rickey replied, "I want a ballplayer with guts enough not to fight back." Robinson said he could be that player.

Robinson spent 1946 playing with the Montreal Royals, a Dodger minor league team. In his first game, he hit a three-run homer, and throughout the season he played well enough to prove he deserved a shot at the majors. That chance came in 1947. On April 15, Robinson started at first base for the Brooklyn Dodgers. That day, he became the first African-American to play professional baseball with whites since the 1880s. Robinson went hitless, but he bunted and reached second base on an error and scored a run in his team's 5–3 victory. Afterward, he told a reporter, "I was comfortable on the field. The Brooklyn players were swell and they were encouraging all the way." His teammates, for the most part, accepted Robinson, and so did the Brooklyn fans. Players and fans in other cities, however, were not so kind.

When the Dodgers played in Philadelphia, the Phillies taunted Robinson, daring him to lash out. Some members of the St. Louis Cardinals threatened to go on strike if Robinson played on their field. The players changed their minds after the league president said he would ban them from baseball if they refused to play. Opposing pitchers threw at Robinson, and other

## BY THE NUMBERS

*Jackie Robinson's career statistics for most offensive categories*

| Year | G | AB | H | 2B | 3B | HR | R | RBI | BB | AVG |
|------|------|------|------|-----|-----|-----|-----|-----|-----|------|
| 1947 | 151 | 590 | 175 | 31 | 5 | 12 | 125 | 48 | 74 | .297 |
| 1948 | 147 | 574 | 170 | 38 | 8 | 12 | 108 | 85 | 57 | .296 |
| 1949 | 156 | 593 | 203 | 38 | 12 | 16 | 122 | 124 | 86 | .342 |
| 1950 | 144 | 518 | 170 | 39 | 4 | 14 | 99 | 81 | 80 | .328 |
| 1951 | 153 | 548 | 185 | 33 | 7 | 19 | 106 | 88 | 79 | .338 |
| 1952 | 149 | 510 | 157 | 17 | 3 | 19 | 104 | 75 | 106 | .308 |
| 1953 | 136 | 484 | 159 | 34 | 7 | 12 | 109 | 95 | 74 | .329 |
| 1954 | 124 | 386 | 120 | 22 | 4 | 15 | 62 | 59 | 63 | .311 |
| 1955 | 105 | 317 | 81 | 6 | 2 | 8 | 51 | 36 | 61 | .256 |
| 1956 | 117 | 357 | 98 | 15 | 2 | 10 | 61 | 43 | 60 | .275 |
| Totals | 1,382 | 4,877 | 1,518 | 273 | 54 | 137 | 947 | 734 | 740 | .311 |

players tried to cut him with their spikes. Robinson even received death threats from fans.

Despite the hatred directed at him, Robinson kept his cool and played well. He also attracted fans, including African-Americans who came by the thousands to watch him play. Robinson finished the season hitting .297, and he led the National League in stolen bases with twenty-nine. He was named the Rookie of the Year in 1947, and two years later he was named the league's Most Valuable Player.

## A Lasting Legacy

Robinson played ten seasons with the Dodgers, finishing his career with a .311 average. In 1962, he was elected to the Baseball Hall of Fame. Robinson's speed and hitting talent were enough to earn him a place in the Hall of Fame, but perhaps his greatest achievement came off the field. Robinson inspired other African-Americans to strive for better treatment in society. Martin Luther King Jr. was a leader in the civil rights movement of the 1950s and 1960s, which fought for equal rights for blacks. King said, "Jackie made my work much less difficult." Robinson died in 1972, and he is still honored for the courage it took to break baseball's color barrier.

*Robinson scoring a winning run in June 1952 against the Chicago Cubs.*

### CHEERS FOR JACKIE

In his autobiography, *I Never Had It Made,* Jackie Robinson remembered the support he received during his first season with the Dodgers:

*Children of all races came to the stands. The very young seemed to have no hangup at all about my being black. They just wanted me to be good, to deliver, to win. . . . I don't think I'll ever forget the small, shrill voice of a tiny white kid who, in the midst of a racially tense atmosphere during an early game in a Dixie town, cried out, "Attaboy, Jackie." It broke the tension and made me feel I had to succeed.*

*The black and the young were my cheering squads. But also there were people—neither black nor young—people of all races and faiths and in all parts of the country, people who couldn't care less about my race.*

# THE OLD MAN MAKES IT

## Satchel Paige Becomes Baseball's Oldest Rookie

"Don't look back," Leroy "Satchel" Paige once said. "Something might be gaining on you." That was part of Paige's legendary strategy for staying young, along—so he claimed—with never running and avoiding fried meat. Paige took his own advice and played baseball into his fifties. Paige had a "rubber arm"—he could pitch countless innings every season and play with little rest. If he had been white, Paige might have collected the most impressive records ever for a major league pitcher. Paige, however, played most of his career before Jackie Robinson broke baseball's color barrier in 1947.

*Satchel Paige toiled as a star pitcher in the Negro Leagues for decades before becoming baseball's oldest rookie in the majors.*

Paige began his career in the Negro Leagues during the 1920s. Tall and thin, Paige was as much an entertainer as an athlete. He gave his pitches nicknames, such as the "two-hump blooper" for his change-up. His fastballs came in different speeds and moved in different ways. Paige could start a game one day and then come in from the bullpen a few days later. No matter when he pitched or how he threw, Paige had amazing control.

## Approaching the Color Barrier

White baseball fans learned about Paige in 1934, when he and other Negro League stars toured with a group of major league all-stars led by pitcher Dizzy Dean. "Old Diz," of the St. Louis Cardinals, had just won thirty games and was one of the best pitchers in the majors. In 1934 and 1935, Paige faced Dean six times and won four. Dean was impressed, calling Paige "the best pitcher I [have] ever see[n]."

Paige continued to pitch in the Negro Leagues while also playing in the Caribbean and Mexico during the winters. He also appeared in other exhibition games with major leaguers. Paige attracted fans wherever he pitched, and he made more money than many white baseball stars. Still, Paige wanted to play in the majors. That chance finally came after Jackie Robinson joined the Brooklyn Dodgers in 1947.

Few baseball fans knew who Robinson was when he first signed with the Dodgers.

*Dizzy Dean, one of the major leagues' top pitchers, toured with Paige and other pitchers from the Negro Leagues in 1934.*

Everyone, however, knew Paige, and some sportswriters thought he should have had the chance to break the color barrier. So did Paige. "I got those boys thinking about having Negroes in the majors," he wrote in his autobiography. "But when they got one, it wasn't me."

### BY THE NUMBERS

*Some of Satchel Paige's regular-season pitching statistics for his years in the majors*

| Year | Team | W | L | CG | SV | SHO | SO | BB | ERA |
|------|------|---|---|----|----|-----|-----|-----|------|
| 1948 | Indians | 6 | 1 | 3 | 1 | 2 | 45 | 25 | 2.48 |
| 1949 | Indians | 4 | 7 | 1 | 5 | 0 | 54 | 33 | 3.04 |
| 1951 | Browns | 3 | 4 | 0 | 5 | 0 | 48 | 29 | 4.7 |
| 1952 | Browns | 12 | 10 | 3 | 10 | 2 | 91 | 57 | 3.07 |
| 1953 | Browns | 3 | 9 | 0 | 11 | 0 | 51 | 39 | 3.5 |
| 1965 | A's | 0 | 0 | 0 | 0 | 0 | 1 | 0 | 0.00 |
| Totals | | 28 | 31 | 7 | 32 | 4 | 290 | 183 | 3.29 |

*Satchel Paige (left) with Larry Doby, the first African-American to play in the American League.*

was the oldest rookie ever in the major leagues, and he proved that he could still pitch. He made his first appearance on July 9, walking slowly from the bullpen to relieve Indians' starter Bob Lemon. "I wasn't nervous exactly," he later wrote, "but I was as close to that feelin' as I could be." Paige threw two scoreless innings and finished the season 6–1, with an earned run average of 2.48. With Paige's help, the Indians went on to win the World Series against the Boston Braves.

## Oldest Rookie

Paige finally made it to the majors in 1948 when he signed a contract with the Cleveland Indians. Cleveland already had Larry Doby, the first African-American to play in the American League. Paige, however, stirred more interest, because of his fame and his age. He was also the majors' first African-American pitcher.

By most reports, Paige was forty-two when he joined Cleveland. Some people claim he was even older, perhaps forty-eight. In any case, he

Paige played one more year with the Indians, left the majors in 1950, and then returned to play for the St. Louis Browns in 1951. His best season was 1952, when he won twelve games and saved ten. Paige made one last major league appearance in 1965. At the age of fifty-nine—or maybe sixty-five—Paige pitched three shutout innings for the Kansas City A's. In 1971, a special committee dedicated to Negro League baseball selected Paige for the Hall of Fame.

Most white baseball fans never got to see the best of Satchel Paige, when he won thirty games a season in the Negro Leagues or shut out opponents for sixty-four consecutive innings. Still, they saw that even in his forties, Paige was a major league talent.

*Paige's last appearance as a big-league pitcher was for the Kansas City A's in 1965.*

## A MASTER OF CONTROL

In his autobiography, *Maybe I'll Pitch Forever,* Satchel Paige described his tryout for the Cleveland Indians in 1948:

*"Can you still throw like you used to?" Mr. Lou [Boudreau] asked me.*

*"I got as fast a ball as anyone pitchin' now, but I got to admit it's not half as fast as it used to be. But I can still pitch it where I want to."*

*"Can you do that against major leaguers?" Mr. Lou asked me.*

*"Don't you worry about that. The plate's the same size up here." . . .*

*Mr. Lou got him a catcher's mitt and went behind the plate. I just tossed a couple real easy and then I started firing. . . .*

*"That's some control, Satch," he told me. "You didn't miss the strike zone more'n four times out of fifty. Those that missed were only an inch or two off the plate, too." . . .*

*It was just like that. Just that easy. As easy as it'd been for me to pitch all those years.*

*I was in the major leagues. The old man'd made it.*

# THE LOUDEST SHOT

## Bobby Thomson's Home Run Gives the New York Giants the Pennant

*Bobby Thomson doing his part to get the Giants back on track by tagging Ralph Kiner in an August 1951 matchup against the Pittsburgh Pirates.*

In 1951, the National League had two teams in New York City: the Brooklyn Dodgers and the New York Giants. Over the years, the two teams had built up a strong rivalry, though during the 1940s, the Dodgers were the better team, winning the pennant three times. The Giants, however, showed improvement in 1950, finishing with their best record in almost a decade.

The 1951 Giants featured pitcher Sal "the Barber" Maglie, known for throwing close to hitters' heads. The center fielder was a rookie named Willie Mays, blessed with speed, power, and a tremendous arm. Monte Irvin was another hard-hitting outfielder, and third baseman Bobby Thomson added extra slugging punch. Managing the team was the feisty Leo Durocher, who had once played for and managed the Dodgers. His move to the Giants branded him a traitor in Brooklyn.

Despite their high hopes entering 1951, something went wrong for the Giants—horribly wrong. They started the season with a win, then lost eleven in a row. By August 12, they were thirteen games behind the Dodgers, who led the league, but that day, the Giants swept a doubleheader, offering a glimmer of hope that their season would not end when the playoffs began.

## Back in the Race

A few days later, New York opened a three-game series against the Dodgers at home. The Giants won all three games, and by August 22, they had won ten in a row and cut Brooklyn's lead to seven and a half games. The winning streak ended at sixteen games, with the Giants just five games behind.

At the end of August, New York lost two out of three to the Pittsburgh Pirates, pushing them back to seven games behind. The Giants faced the Dodgers for their first two games in September, beating them easily each time. When the two teams met again a week later, the

*Thomson running down a pop-up off the bat of Gil Hodges during the 1951 playoff series against the Dodgers.*

Dodgers' lead had nudged back up to five and a half games. Said one Dodger, "It still didn't really enter our minds at that time that those guys really had a chance to win." The Giants split the series, losing a chance to gain ground.

With just a little more than a week left in the season, the Dodger lead was four and a half games. Now the Dodgers seemed sure to win. The Giants, however, went on another winning streak, taking their last seven games. Meanwhile, the Dodgers struggled, winning only three before the last day of the season. By then, the Giants had pulled ahead by half a game. The Dodgers needed extra innings to win their last game, tying New York's record of 96–58. The two teams prepared to play a best-of-three series to determine the National League's pennant winner. A New York sportswriter noted that the city went "quietly mad trying figure out which . . . team to root for."

*Delirious New York Giants fans reacting as Thomson sprints for the locker room following his pennant-winning home run.*

## Thomson's Big Blast

The Giants won the first game, 3–1, with Thomson and Irvin hitting home runs. The Dodgers fought back to win the second game. The pennant would come down to the final play-off game.

In this last game, the Giants' Maglie faced the Dodgers' Don Newcombe, a twenty-game winner. Both men pitched well, and the score was tied at 1 after seven innings. In the top of the eighth, the Dodgers used several hits, a walk, and a wild pitch to score three runs, taking a commanding 4–1 lead. Newcombe held the Giants scoreless in the eighth. The Dodgers did not score in the ninth. Before his team came up in the bottom of the inning, Durocher spoke to the Giants. "It's not over yet," he said. "Let's go out there and give them all we got."

### BY THE NUMBERS

*Bobby Thomson's major batting statistics for the 1951 season*

| G | AB | H | 2B | 3B | HR | RBI | R | AVG |
|---|-----|-----|----|----|----|-----|----|------|
| 148 | 518 | 152 | 27 | 8 | 32 | 101 | 89 | .293 |

Alvin Dark led off for the Giants and singled to right. Don Mueller followed with another single, moving Dark to third. Irvin fouled out, but Whitey Lockman doubled home Dark. Mueller reached third but had to leave the game with an injury and was replaced by pinch runner Clint Hartung. The next batter was Bobby Thomson. The Dodgers brought in reliever Ralph Branca to face him. The first pitch was a called strike. On the next pitch, Thomson connected and drilled a line drive to left. Leaving the bat, the ball looked like it might hit the wall for a double. Instead, it cleared the fence, giving Thomson a three-run homer and the Giants their first pennant since 1937.

Thomson became an instant hero with New York fans, and his homer was nicknamed "the shot heard 'round the world." The Giants' winning ways, however, ended in the World Series, as the New York Yankees beat them in six games. Still, Thomson's home run was never forgotten. Some people have called it the most memorable home run ever, as it capped the Giants' amazing comeback, one of the greatest in sports history.

*Thomson sharing the celebration following his historic homer with Giants owner Horace Stoneham (left) and manager Leo Durocher.*

## A WINNING MOMENT

Years after his historic game-winning homer, Bobby Thomson recalled the moment:

*Then I realized Branca was ready to pitch. I took the first one down the middle, a ball I should have swung at. I waited again. Branca's pitch came in high and inside . . . I was quick with my hands. After I hit it, I watched it go. At first I was sure it was a home run, then I saw the ball start to sink when I got halfway to first. A look again, and I realized it was disappearing into the stands. Then I knew we were all right. I jumped and skipped around those bases like I was half nuts.*

# YANKEE PERFECTION

## Don Larsen Throws a Perfect Game in the 1956 World Series

"Perfect" means just one thing to a major league pitcher: twenty-seven batters up, and twenty-seven batters down. No hits, no walks, no errors, no batters hit by a pitch. A no-hitter is hard enough to achieve, but a perfect game is the rarest event in baseball. Only sixteen pitchers have ever thrown one—and only Don Larsen has ever thrown one in a World Series.

In 1956, Larsen was not the winningest pitcher on the New

*Don Larsen with his battery mate, Yankee catcher Yogi Berra.*

*Don Larsen throwing in the 1956 World Series.*

York Yankees. Appearing as both a starter and a reliever, he finished the regular season with an 11–5 record. Larsen started Game 2 of the World Series that year against the Brooklyn Dodgers, but he didn't last two innings. Before his next start in Game 5, Larsen told a reporter, "I'm gonna beat those guys tomorrow." Then he added, "And I'm just liable to throw a no-hitter."

## A Perfect Start

It was a chilly afternoon at Yankee Stadium on October 8. Larsen got the Dodgers out in order in the first inning, and Brooklyn starter Sal Maglie matched him. For three innings, neither pitcher allowed a man to reach base. Then, with two outs in the bottom of the fourth, Maglie gave up the game's first hit, a home run to right by Mickey Mantle. In the top of the fifth, Brooklyn first baseman Gil Hodges threatened to match Mantle's blast with one of his own, but the ball stayed in the park and Mantle tracked it down in center field.

In the top of the sixth, Yankee second baseman Billy Martin wrapped his glove around two pop-ups for the first two outs, and then Larsen struck out Maglie. In the bottom of the inning, the Yankees added a second run, though the way Larsen was pitching, one seemed plenty. The Dodgers went down in order again in the seventh, and after the inning, Larsen asked Mantle if he thought Larsen could get a no-hitter. Mantle was surprised by the question, since baseball players usually believe it's bad luck to talk about a no-hitter while it's happening. Larsen obviously was not worried about this superstition.

*The scoreboard tells the tale as Larsen delivers the final pitch of his perfect game.*

## Down on Strikes

In the eighth, Larsen got a groundout, a strikeout, and a lineout. The fans at Yankee Stadium buzzed with excitement when he stepped out to pitch in the ninth. They knew Larsen needed only three more outs to make history. The first Dodger batter was Carl Furillo. He hit a ball deep to right, but outfielder Hank Bauer snared it. Next up was Roy Campanella, who hit an easy grounder to second.

Maglie was due to hit next, but pinch hitter Dale Mitchell stepped up instead.

Mitchell was a tough hitter who rarely struck out. After the game, Larsen said, "I was so weak in the knees out there in the ninth, I thought I was going to faint." Yet he didn't show his nerves to Mitchell. After throwing the first pitch for a ball, Larsen came back with a called strike. On the next pitch, a fastball, Mitchell swung and missed. Then he fouled off a pitch. The next time Larsen threw, Mitchell tried to check his swing on a ball that seemed low and outside, but umpire Babe Pinelli called strike three. The next thing Larsen knew, catcher Yogi

### BY THE NUMBERS

*The line on Don Larsen for his perfect game*

| IP | H | R | ER | W | SO |
|----|---|---|----|---|----|
| 9  | 0 | 0 | 0  | 0 | 7  |

Berra was leaping into his arms, and the other Yankees rushed over to celebrate the only perfect game in World Series history.

Larsen was an instant star after that performance. The rest of his career, however, did not go so well. He won just ten games the next season, and he retired in 1967 with more career losses than wins. Still, for one day, Larsen was perfect. He later said, "I still find it hard to believe. . . . It's almost like a dream, like something that happened to somebody else."

*At the end of his perfect game, Larsen is mobbed by Yogi Berra and other members of the Yankee team.*

## THE LARSEN PITCHING STYLE

A *New York Times* article from October 9, 1956, quoted Don Larsen on a new pitching style that helped him throw his perfect game:

*At the time I was using the wind-up I was tipping off my pitches . . . no matter what I threw [an opposing coach] knew what was coming. So I went to [Yankee pitching coach] Jim Turner and asked his permission to drop the wind-up. . . . It gives me better control. It takes nothing off my fastball and keeps the batters tense. They have to be ready every second. And don't forget, no coach can "read" the pitch in advance.*

# HAMMERING A NEW RECORD

## Hank Aaron Breaks Babe Ruth's Career Home-Run Record

In 1927, Babe Ruth belted sixty home runs, beating the record of fifty-nine he had set six years earlier. Ruth's new record stood until 1961, when Roger Maris hit sixty-one. Ruth's career home-run total of 714, however, seemed out of reach for other hitters. Until the 1970s, only a handful of sluggers reached 500, and Willie Mays and Hank Aaron were the only players besides Ruth to hit more than 600. When Mays retired in 1973, his career total stood at 660, and the Babe's record still held. Aaron, however, showed that the old sports saying is true: Records are made to be broken.

*Hank Aaron played for the Braves during most of his career, first in Milwaukee and then in Atlanta. He finished his career back in Milwaukee with the Brewers.*

Playing for the Milwaukee Braves, "Hammerin' Hank" hit his first major league home run in 1954 and finished his rookie season with thirteen. His batting talent exploded in 1957, when Aaron led the National League with forty-four homers and he was named the league's most valuable player (MVP). Over the years, Aaron hit for both power and average, becoming one of the most dependable hitters in the game.

### Chasing "the Babe"

In July 1968, Aaron joined the elite 500 home-run club. It took less than three more seasons for

*For decades, Babe Ruth's career home-run record of 714 stood fast.*

Aaron to reach 600 homers. As Aaron finished 1971 with forty-seven home runs, his personal best for a single season, some people began to wonder if Aaron could pass Ruth's career record. The next year, Aaron belted thirty-four, and in 1973 he added forty more for a career total of 673 four-baggers. At that point, the baseball world knew Aaron could break Ruth's record, as long as he stayed healthy.

Most fans cheered for Aaron, hoping he could set a new record. Others, however, did not like the idea of an African-American passing Ruth, who was still considered the game's first national hero. Aaron received many racist letters as he approached home run number 714. He decided that "the best way to shut up the kind of people who wrote those . . . letters was to have a good year. The letters, I would say, inspired me."

## 715 and Beyond

Aaron's 700th homer came in July 1973. At age thirty-nine, he finished the season with forty home runs, marking the eighth time in his career he reached that level. He also had 713 career home runs. Aaron was disappointed that he didn't break Ruth's record that year. In the off-season he married Billye Williams, his second wife. Later Aaron wrote that he spent the winter thinking about the first pitch he would see in 1974, "even lying on the beach in Jamaica with my new bride."

## BY THE NUMBERS

*Hank Aaron's home run totals for his twenty-three-year career*

| Year | Home Runs |
|------|-----------|
| 1954 | 13 |
| 1955 | 27 |
| 1956 | 26 |
| 1957 | 44 |
| 1958 | 30 |
| 1959 | 39 |
| 1960 | 40 |
| 1961 | 34 |
| 1962 | 45 |
| 1963 | 44 |
| 1964 | 24 |
| 1965 | 32 |
| 1966 | 44 |
| 1967 | 39 |
| 1968 | 29 |
| 1969 | 44 |
| 1970 | 38 |
| 1971 | 47 |
| 1972 | 34 |
| 1973 | 40 |
| 1974 | 20 |
| 1975 | 12 |
| 1976 | 10 |
| Total: | 755 |

*Aaron hitting home run number 714 on April 4, 1974, and tying Babe Ruth's record.*

Once the next season started, Aaron did not wait long to tie Ruth's record. The Braves opened the season in Cincinnati. In his first at-bat, Aaron smacked a 3–1 pitch for a three-run homer. The crowd hoped for the record breaker that day, but Aaron went hitless the rest of the game. He sat out the Braves' next game, and Braves manager Eddie Matthews wanted him out of the third game as well, so Aaron's next shot at the record would come at home in Atlanta. Instead, major league commissioner Bowie Kuhn ordered Matthews to play Aaron. The commissioner was criticized for this heavy-handed move, and Aaron went zero for three in the last game of the series.

On April 8, nearly 54,000 fans crowded Atlanta's Fulton County Stadium for the Braves' first home game, along with a television crew hoping to broadcast a historic moment to 30 million Americans watching at home. Among the people attending the game was Georgia governor—and future president—Jimmy Carter. Commissioner Kuhn, however, was nowhere in sight.

Batting in the second inning, Aaron had no chance to swing for the fences, and he drew a walk. The next time up, however, Aaron saw the pitch he wanted. Connecting on a fastball, he sent the pitch into the Braves' bullpen, where reliever Tom House caught Aaron's 715th home run. The crowd went wild as Aaron circled the bases, and the cheering lasted for ten minutes. His parents greeted him on the field, and later Aaron joked, "I never knew that my mother could hug so tight."

Aaron finished the season with eighteen home runs. After the season, he was traded to the Milwaukee Brewers, and he finished his amazing career in the city where it began. When Aaron retired in 1976, he had 755 home runs. He also held several other career records, including most extra-base hits and games played. After breaking one of the greatest sports records of all time, Aaron was an obvious choice for the Hall of Fame.

*Aaron's teammates gather to congratulate him after he belts his record-breaking 715th career home run on April 8, 1974.*

## A SURPRISING SHOT

In his autobiography, *I Had a Hammer*, Hank Aaron wrote about hitting his 715th home run:

*I hit it squarely, although not well enough that I knew it was gone. The ball shot out on a line over the shortstop, Bill Russell, who bent his knees as if he were going to jump up and catch it. That was one of the differences between me and Ruth: he made outfielders look up at the sky, and I made shortstops bend their knees. . . .*

*The ball kept going. It surprised [Dodger outfielder Bill Buckner], and it surprised me. I'm still not sure I hit that ball hard enough for it to go out. I don't know—maybe I did but I was so keyed up that I couldn't feel it. Anyway, something carried the ball into the bullpen and about the time I got to first base I realized I was the all-time home run king of baseball.*

# NOLAN'S NO-NO'S

## Nolan Ryan Throws His Seventh No-Hitter

*Nolan Ryan, shown here acknowledging an ovation from the crowd, led the American League in strikeouts during his first season with the California Angels.*

New York City is a long way from the small town of Alvin, Texas, where pitcher Nolan Ryan first played baseball as a kid. Ryan said he was awed when he went to the Big Apple in 1966 to pitch for the New York Mets. During his career, Ryan

stirred even greater awe in the batters who tried to hit his 100-mile-per-hour (161-kilometer-per-hour) fastball, a blazing trail of white known as "the Ryan Express."

With that fastball, Ryan struck out 5,714

hitters, the most ever by a major league pitcher, and won 324 games. That pitch, along with a hard curveball, also made Ryan baseball's no-hit king—the author of more no-hitters than any other pitcher in the big leagues.

## Premier Pitcher

Early in his career with the Mets, Ryan threw fast, but he was also inconsistent. In five seasons with New York, he lost more games than he won. In 1972, Ryan went to the California Angels, where his career blossomed. That first season, he had 329 strikeouts, leading the American League. The next year, he threw his first no-hitter, striking out twelve Kansas City Royals in a 3–0 victory. Ryan tossed a second "no-no" later that year and one more each of the next two seasons to rack up an astonishing four no-hitters in three seasons.

No-hitter number five didn't come for six more years, but it was a milestone, breaking the old record for career no-hitters held by Sandy Koufax. In 1981, pitching for the Houston Astros, Ryan no-hit the Los Angeles Dodgers, 5–0. "That one was real special for me," Ryan said. "It was at home in the Astrodome, where the fans have always been good to me. . . . And it was during a pennant race, in a game we needed to win."

During the next few seasons in Houston, Ryan struggled a bit. He still struck out batters and won games, but his statistics were not as impressive. Part of the problem was physical, as

*The Dodgers' Sandy Koufax showing off the scoreboard after his second no-hitter.*

he suffered with a sore elbow in 1986. When the elbow recovered, Ryan returned to his old form. By 1989, however, the Astros weren't willing to pay the high salary Ryan deserved as one of baseball's greatest pitchers. Ryan went to the Texas Rangers. In 1990, his second season in Texas, he threw his sixth no-hitter. At age forty-three, Ryan became the oldest pitcher to accomplish that feat.

## Lucky Seven

After that successful season, which included his 300th career win, Ryan was ready to keep pitch-

*Ryan and his Texas teammates celebrating his sixth no-hitter.*

ing. On May 1, 1991, the Toronto Blue Jays came to Arlington, home of the Rangers, and Ryan was on the mound. He walked Kelly Gruber in the first but got out of the inning. In the sixth inning, Manny Lee hit a tricky blooper into cen-ter field, but Rangers outfielder Gary Pettis tracked it down and nabbed it on the fly. Through the first seven innings, Ryan did not give up a hit and struck out thirteen batters.

Toronto outfielder Mark Whiten led off

## BY THE NUMBERS

### Nolan Ryan's seven no-hit games

| May 15, 1973 | California Angels 3, Kansas City Royals 0 | 12 strikeouts |
|---|---|---|
| July 15, 1973 | California Angels 6, Detroit Tigers 0 | 17 strikeouts |
| September 28, 1974 | California Angels 4, Minnesota Twins 0 | 15 strikeouts |
| June 1, 1975 | California Angels 1, Baltimore Orioles 0 | 9 strikeouts |
| September 26, 1981 | Houston Astros 5, Los Angeles Dodgers 0 | 11 strikeouts |
| June 11, 1990 | Texas Rangers 5, Oakland A's 0 | 14 strikeouts |
| May 1, 1991 | Texas Rangers 3, Toronto Blue Jays 0 | 16 strikeouts |

the eighth inning. By now, more fans had flooded into the stadium, as they learned Ryan was throwing a no-hitter. Whiten hit a hard line drive to right, the best contact the Jays had made all night, but Ruben Sierra was right there to catch it. Ryan easily retired the next two batters.

In the ninth, Manny Lee led off for the Blue Jays and grounded out. Devon White followed with another weak grounder. The fans cheered for Ryan as Roberto Alomar stepped up to the plate. The Jays' second baseman worked the count to 2–2. Then Ryan fired a 93-mile-per-hour (150-km-per-hour) fastball. Alomar swung—and missed. The scoreboard told the story for Toronto: no runs, no hits. Ryan had thrown his seventh and last no-hitter, finishing the game with sixteen strikeouts and just two walks.

Years later, Ryan called that game his greatest thrill. "I was forty-four years old and that was probably the best game I ever pitched." Ryan also noted that Alomar was the son of Sandy Alomar, who had played second base behind him during his first two no-hitters. In a career that touched on each of the last four decades of the twentieth century, Ryan had become the only pitcher to ever no-hit two generations of ballplayers!

Ryan retired in 1993 and was elected to the Hall of Fame in 1999. In the words of his former teammate and fellow Hall of Famer Tom Seaver, Ryan will always rank "as the most overpowering pitcher in history."

## PITCHING THROUGH PAIN

In his autobiography, *Miracle Man*, Nolan Ryan recounted how he felt before he pitched his last no-hitter:

*I didn't expect to pitch well at all that night. I woke up with a sore back and took painkillers all day before leaving for the park. I went through extra stretching and exercises and even wore a heating pad during the scouting meeting where we go over the hitters. That wasn't the only thing wrong with me. While I was warming up I told Tom House, ". . . I feel old today. My back hurts, my finger hurts, my ankle hurts, everything hurts." Scar tissue tore open on the middle finger of my pitching hand in the bullpen, and I had one of my worst warm-ups ever. . . .*

*Before the game, Bobby [Valentine, the Texas manager] asked me how my back was. I told him that it was stiff. He said, "How will it be once you start pitching?" I said, "It'll be history." Adrenaline always takes over when I'm on the mound, and it did again. . . . My stuff was surprisingly good, considering all that was wrong with me that day.*

*Ryan threw his sixth and seventh no-hitters as a Texas Ranger.*

# THE NEW IRON MAN

## Cal Ripken Jr. Plays in His 2,131st Consecutive Game— and Then Some

*Baltimore's Cal Ripken Jr. gets an "Attaboy" from his dad, Baltimore third-base coach Cal Ripken Sr., after hitting a home run against the New York Yankees in September 1982.*

One day in 1925, New York Yankees first baseman Wally Pipp asked to sit out a game, complaining of a headache. A rookie named Lou Gehrig filled in for him, starting a string of 2,130 consecutive games played and a career that guaranteed the "Iron Horse" a place in the Hall of Fame. Only a disease called amyotrophic lateral sclerosis (now sometimes called "Lou Gehrig's disease") kept Gehrig from playing longer.

Fifty-seven years later, a young player for the Baltimore Orioles earned his chance to play every day. In 1982, at age twenty-one, Cal Ripken Jr. was a rookie entering his first full season in the majors. On May 29, he sat out the second game of a doubleheader, but the next day he returned to the lineup. Ripken did not miss another game for sixteen seasons, easily breaking Gehrig's endurance record and setting a new standard for dedication to the game of baseball.

### Born to Play

Ripken was born in 1960 in Maryland. His father, Cal Sr., was a minor-league baseball player for the Orioles. Although

*The legendary Lou Gehrig played 2,130 consecutive games—all of them in a New York Yankees uniform.*

he never made the "bigs," Ripken Sr. was knowledgeable about baseball and the Orioles used him as a scout and a coach. Ripken Jr. worked as a batboy for several of his father's minor league teams. He also had the chance to field grounders and fly balls with the players, and he learned the game well. Ripken was already committed to playing as much as he could. His mother once said, "I wish I had a nickel for every time I heard, 'Just one more game, Mom.'"

As a teen, Ripken knew he wanted to play professional baseball, and in 1978 the Orioles signed him to a contract. Ripken had been a star pitcher in high school, but he focused on playing infield in the pros. In August 1981, Ripken played his first major league game, appearing as a pinch runner. The rest of the year, he saw limited playing time and had a grand total of five hits, all singles. "By this time," he wrote in his autobiography, "my confidence was sort of beat down."

The Orioles, however, gave Ripken another chance to prove himself. He started the 1982 season as the third baseman and then moved to short. At the plate, he belted a home run on opening day and hit well the whole year. Ripken

*Throughout his career with the Baltimore Orioles, Ripken distinguished himself as a solid, heads-up infielder.*

finished the season with a .264 average, twenty-eight homers, and ninety-three RBIs—impressive enough to earn him Rookie of the Year honors.

## Excellence Every Day

The next season, Ripken led the American League in hits, doubles, and runs scored, and also hit twenty-seven home runs and drove in 102. He was named the league's MVP and helped the Orioles win the World Series. Throughout the 1980s, Ripken was a consistent hitter and a great fielder, usually leading the league in most assists for a shortstop. Not only did Ripken not miss a game during this time, but for almost five seasons he played every inning in every Orioles game. Starting in 1983, he was elected to play in the All-Star game nineteen times.

Ripken's best season in the field was 1990, when he set nine records, including fewest errors by a shortstop—just three. At the plate, his best year was 1991. He hit .323, with thirty-four homers and 114 RBIs. That season he also won his first Gold Glove Award as the league's best-fielding shortstop. Ripken's final honor for the year was his second MVP award.

At the start of that 1991 season, Ripken

had played in more than 1,500 consecutive games, second only to Gehrig, with his incredible 2,130 games in a row. As Ripken continued to play every day, even with sprained ankles and twisted knees, baseball fans began doing the math. At age thirty, Ripken might still have enough years in him to break the Iron Horse's record. Game 2,000 came about three and half years later, in August 1994—right before a players' strike ended the season. The magic number of 2,131 was elusive, but it remained within reach and would come the next year—if Ripken remained healthy.

## BY THE NUMBERS

*Cal Ripken's major batting statistics for his career*

| Year | G | AB | R | H | 2B | 3B | HR | RBI | AVG |
|------|-----|--------|-------|-------|-----|----|-----|-------|------|
| 1981 | 23 | 39 | 1 | 5 | 0 | 0 | 0 | 0 | .128 |
| 1982 | 160 | 598 | 90 | 158 | 32 | 5 | 28 | 93 | .264 |
| 1983 | 162 | 663 | 121 | 211 | 47 | 2 | 27 | 102 | .318 |
| 1984 | 162 | 641 | 103 | 195 | 37 | 7 | 27 | 86 | .304 |
| 1985 | 161 | 642 | 116 | 181 | 32 | 5 | 26 | 110 | .282 |
| 1986 | 162 | 627 | 98 | 177 | 35 | 1 | 25 | 81 | .282 |
| 1987 | 162 | 624 | 97 | 157 | 28 | 3 | 27 | 98 | .252 |
| 1988 | 161 | 575 | 87 | 152 | 25 | 1 | 23 | 81 | .264 |
| 1989 | 162 | 646 | 80 | 166 | 30 | 0 | 21 | 93 | .257 |
| 1990 | 161 | 600 | 78 | 150 | 28 | 4 | 21 | 84 | .250 |
| 1991 | 162 | 650 | 99 | 210 | 46 | 5 | 34 | 114 | .323 |
| 1992 | 162 | 637 | 73 | 160 | 29 | 1 | 14 | 72 | .251 |
| 1993 | 162 | 641 | 87 | 165 | 26 | 3 | 24 | 90 | .257 |
| 1994 | 112 | 444 | 71 | 140 | 19 | 3 | 13 | 75 | .315 |
| 1995 | 144 | 550 | 71 | 144 | 33 | 2 | 17 | 88 | .262 |
| 1996 | 163 | 640 | 94 | 178 | 40 | 1 | 26 | 102 | .278 |
| 1997 | 162 | 615 | 79 | 166 | 30 | 0 | 17 | 84 | .270 |
| 1998 | 161 | 601 | 65 | 163 | 27 | 1 | 14 | 61 | .271 |
| 1999 | 86 | 332 | 51 | 113 | 27 | 0 | 18 | 57 | .340 |
| 2000 | 83 | 309 | 43 | 79 | 16 | 0 | 15 | 56 | .256 |
| 2001 | 128 | 477 | 43 | 114 | 16 | 0 | 14 | 68 | .239 |
| Career | 3,001 | 11,551 | 1,647 | 3,184 | 603 | 44 | 431 | 1,695 | .276 |

## The New Iron Horse

At spring training in 1995, fifty reporters and twenty photographers gathered around Ripken. The media attention grew as the season went on. Everyone asked if Ripken knew much about Gehrig and his record. A hardworking guy with a streak of modesty that matched his playing streak, Ripken said no. He wasn't playing to set a record, Ripken explained: "The only comparison [with Gehrig] I could see was our love of playing the game."

On September 5, Ripken played his 2,130th consecutive game. In the sixth inning, he hit a home run to left, giving the fans at Baltimore's Camden Yards another reason to celebrate. The next night, as Ripken took the field, the fans honored him with an ovation. He gave them more to cheer about with a homer in the fourth. But it was after the fifth inning, when the game became official, that the park erupted in cheers and tears for Ripken. For more than ten minutes the fans honored a player who always gave his best on the field.

After the 1995 season, Ripken was given many honors, including being named Male Athlete of the Year by AP and UPI as well as Sportsman of the Year by *Sports Illustrated* and *The Sporting News*. He continued to play every game for the next three years—until September 20, 1998, after 2,632 consecutive games. Ripkin was not injured, but he chose to take himself out of the lineup. As he told Orioles manager Ray Miller, "I think the time is right."

The next season, he hit his 400th career homer, and in 2000 he reached 3,000 total hits. He became just the seventh player to reach both of those milestones. Ripken finally retired after the 2001 season, ending one of the most inspiring sports careers ever. But Ripken could not totally leave behind the game he loved, so he planned to spend much of his time working with youth baseball.

*Ripken takes in the surroundings at Baltimore's Camden Yards on the day he broke Lou Gehrig's consecutive-game playing streak.*

## DO YOUR VERY BEST

Here is part of the speech Cal Ripken made the night he broke Lou Gehrig's record for consecutive games played:

*I know that if Lou Gehrig is looking down on tonight's activities, he isn't concerned with someone's playing more games than he did. Instead, he's viewing tonight as just another example of what's good and right about the great American game. Whether your name is Gehrig or Ripken, or DiMaggio or Robinson, or that of some youngster who picks up his bat or puts on his glove, you are challenged by the game of baseball to do your very best, day in and day out, and that's all I ever tried to do.*

# CLASH OF THE HOME-RUN TITANS

## Mark McGwire and Sammy Sosa Battle for the Home-Run Record

In 1961, New York Yankees teammates Roger Maris and Mickey Mantle chased Babe Ruth's record of sixty home runs in a season. Their pursuit of the Babe added a jolt of excitement to the baseball season—

*Sixty-one in '61: Babe Ruth's single-season record of sixty home runs, set in 1927, stood for thirty-four years before Roger Maris, shown here swinging for the fences in 1961, surpassed that total by one.*

"Mick." In the end, Maris set the new mark with sixty-one, though some baseball fans felt the record was tainted. Ruth had hit sixty when teams played 154 games a season, while in 1961, with more teams in the majors,

in no small part due to the fact that Maris and Mantle played on the same star-studded Yankees team and brought such contrasting styles and personalities to the drama. Mantle, a Yankees stalwart, was outgoing and personable; Maris, a relative newcomer to the Yanks, was more withdrawn and seemed sullen in contrast to the

they played 162. Still, no one could dispute how tough it was to hit sixty or more round-trippers. After Maris did it, no other player would hit more than fifty-two until thirty-six years had passed. In 1997, Mark McGwire smacked fifty-eight while playing for the Oakland A's and the St. Louis Cardinals.

*While battling Mark McGwire in their 1998 race for the single-season record, the Chicago Cubs' Sammy Sosa surpassed both Ruth and Maris with sixty-six home runs of his own.*

sluggers treated baseball fans to an entertaining season in 1998 and sparked the enthusiasm and admiration of people who previously might not have considered themselves fans of the game. Along the way, McGwire and Sosa's home-run rivalry led to mutual respect and friendship.

## The Race Begins

McGwire started the 1998 season on fire, hitting a grand slam in the Cardinals' first game and one homer in each of the next three. By the end of May, "Big Mac" had twenty-seven home runs. One of those gave him 400 for his career; McGwire reached that mark faster than any player in history. Another one of those early blasts traveled 545 feet (166 meters), one of the longest recorded home runs ever.

During that stretch, Sosa hit just thirteen homers, but in June he went on a tear, hitting twenty and setting a new record for most home runs in one month. Sosa joked, "It was a pretty

The next year, McGwire and Sammy Sosa of the Chicago Cubs competed in a season-long duel to beat Maris's record.

McGwire, a huge first baseman, had always been a power hitter, but injuries limited his home-run totals some years. Sosa, who hailed from the Dominican Republic, had played outfield for several teams before landing with the Cubs in 1992, where he emerged as a star. Unlike McGwire, however, his home-run totals never suggested he might one day top Maris. These two good month." By the All-Star game in July, Sosa trailed McGwire by only four homers.

McGwire kept a slim lead in the home-run race until August 16, when Sosa tied him with forty-seven. Three days later, as the Cards and Cubs met in Chicago, Sosa added another, but McGwire hit two to regain the lead. By now, the whole country knew about the race to beat Maris's record, as newspapers kept track of every home run. On August 20, McGwire hit number fifty, becoming the first player to hit fifty or more homers three years in a row. At the end of August, Sosa and McGwire had fifty-five each, and it seemed likely both men would pass Maris. The only questions were, who would finish the season on top, and how high would the final mark be?

## The Record—and More

McGwire started the last month of the season with four round-trippers in two games. McGwire, however, knew Sosa could get hot. "Sammy's a September player," he said, "so you have to watch out for him. It's crunch time— time to make history."

McGwire made history first.

On September 5, he tied Ruth's old record of sixty home runs. Two days later, playing against the Cubs in St. Louis, he tied Maris's record. Then, on September 8, McGwire stepped up against Chicago pitcher Steve Trachsel in the fourth inning. He lifted a fly ball to left, barely clearing the fence. The homer was McGwire's shortest of the season,

*The St. Louis Cardinals' Mark McGwire connects for one of his record-setting seventy home runs.*

but it gave him the home-run record. As the fans cheered and fireworks went off around Busch Stadium, Sosa came in from his position in right field to hug McGwire. Later, McGwire said, "It's an absolutely incredible feeling."

It took McGwire a week to get his next home run. Sosa, meanwhile, hit four to bring his total up to sixty-two. During mid-September, the two sluggers were tied several times as they fought for the lead. On September 26, with just two games to go, each had sixty-six four-baggers. Sosa did not connect over that last weekend, but McGwire went out with a bang, hitting two homers each day and finishing his historic season with seventy. Afterward, Sosa told the press, "I'm real happy for him, because, hey, he's the man." McGwire added, "We're just two guys who really enjoy playing the game. . . . I'm really proud of the things I've done this year with Sammy Sosa."

## HOME-RUN CELEBRATION

*New York Times* reporter Murry Chass described the scene after Mark McGwire hit his sixty-second home run:

> As he ran to first base, McGwire followed the flight of the ball. When he reached first, he missed the base. . . . "That is the first time that I think I missed it," McGwire said.
>
> [First base coach Dave] McKay . . . quickly pointed to the base so that McGwire would go back and touch it. McGwire did, as the fans roared a constant roar, then began trotting toward second. As he rounded the bases, the Cubs' infielders congratulated him.
>
> Just short of home plate, Scott Servais, the Cubs catcher, shook his hand, and McGwire grabbed him around the neck. The Cardinals mobbed McGwire after he stepped on the plate, and Fernando Tatis, the young third baseman . . . leaped on top of the mob to try to reach McGwire. The exuberant McGwire then hugged his teammates individually.

## BY THE NUMBERS

*Month-by-month home-run totals for Mark McGwire and Sammy Sosa during 1998*

|        | McGwire | Sosa |
|--------|---------|------|
| April  | 11      | 6    |
| May    | 16      | 7    |
| June   | 10      | 20   |
| July   | 8       | 9    |
| August | 10      | 13   |
| Sept.  | 15      | 11   |
| Total  | 70      | 66   |

## ANOTHER HOME-RUN RECORD

Mark McGwire's home-run record lasted just three years. In 2001, San Francisco Giants slugger Barry Bonds amazed baseball fans by hitting seventy-three homers. He also set a new record for walks (177) and slugging percentage (.863). McGwire won't have a chance to try to regain the single-season home-run record, however. He announced his retirement at the end of that season.

# Baseball Time Line

**1770s** Americans play a game called "base ball," based on older English games using a ball and stick.

**1846** Two New York teams play the first baseball game using modern rules.

**1869** The Cincinnati Red Stockings become the first professional baseball team.

**1876** The National League forms.

**1901** The American League forms, marking the start of modern professional baseball.

**1903** The Boston Pilgrims of the American League defeat the Pittsburgh Pirates of the National League in the first World Series.

**1927** Babe Ruth hits sixty home runs.

**1933** The first All-Star game is played in Chicago, with the American League winning, 4–2.

**1939** Lou Gehrig ends his streak of 2,130 consecutive games played.

**1941** Joe DiMaggio hits in fifty-six consecutive games; Ted Williams finishes the season with a .406 average.

**1947** Jackie Robinson breaks the color barrier in major league baseball when he appears in a Brooklyn Dodgers uniform.

**1948** At age forty-two, Satchel Paige plays for the Cleveland Indians, becoming the major leagues' oldest rookie and its first African-American pitcher.

**1951** Bobby Thomson hits a ninth-inning home run, which gives the New York Giants the National League pennant.

**1956** Don Larsen pitches the only perfect game in World Series history.

**1961** Roger Maris hits sixty-one home runs, breaking Babe Ruth's single-season record.

**1969** Each major league splits into two divisions, and a league championship series decides the pennant winner.

**1973** Nolan Ryan throws his first two no-hitters.

**1974** Hank Aaron hits his 715th career home run, breaking Babe Ruth's lifetime record.

**1991** Nolan Ryan throws his seventh—and last—no-hitter.

**1994** A disagreement between owners and players leads to a cancelation of the last two months of the season; each league adds a third division and includes a third and a fourth team in the postseason playoffs.

**1995** Cal Ripken Jr. breaks Lou Gehrig's career record for consecutive games played.

**1998** Mark McGwire and Sammy Sosa compete to break Roger Maris's record of sixty-one home runs; McGwire finishes with seventy and Sosa with sixty-six.

**2001** Cal Ripken retires; Barry Bonds of the San Francisco Giants breaks McGwire's home-run record, finishing the season with seventy-three.

# To Learn More

## BOOKS

Christopher, Matt. *Great Moments in Baseball History.* Boston: Little, Brown, 1995.

DeAngelis, Gina. *Jackie Robinson.* Philadelphia: Chelsea House, 2001.

Nicholson, Lois. *Nolan Ryan.* New York: Chelsea House, 1996.

Ripken, Cal Jr., and Mike Bryan. *My Story.* Adapted by Mike Gutman. New York: Dial Books for Young Readers, 1997.

Ritter, Lawrence S. *The Story of Baseball.* 3rd rev. Foreword by Ted Williams. New York: William Morrow, 1999.

Stewart, Mark, and Mike Kennedy. *Home Run Heroes: Mark McGwire & Sammy Sosa.* Brookfield, Conn.: Millbrook, 1999.

Uschan, Michael V. *Home Run Kings.* San Diego: Lucent, 2000.

## INTERNET SITES

### The Baseball Almanac
*www.baseball-almanac.com/*
Filled with facts and stats on every player; also has quotes from some of the greatest stars and reviews of every World Series.

### The Baseball Archive
*www.baseball1.com/*
Includes articles about former and current players, columns from well-known sportswriters, and an encyclopedia.

### Baseball Reference.com
*www.baseball-reference.com*
Another site devoted to stats, records, and the history of the game.

### The National Baseball Hall of Fame and Museum
*www.baseballhalloffame.org/index.htm*
Has biographies of every member and a changing lineup of online exhibits on the history of the game.

### Negro League Baseball
*www.negroleaguebaseball.com*
Honors the players of the old Negro Leagues, with player profiles and news about current tributes to past teams.

# Index

## ABOUT THE AUTHOR

*As an editor at* Weekly Reader *for six years, Michael Burgan created educational material for an interactive online service and wrote on current events. Now a freelance author, Michael has written more than thirty books, primarily for children and young adults. These include biographies of Secretary of State Madeleine Albright, Presidents John Adams and John F. Kennedy, and astronaut John Glenn. His other historical writings include two volumes in a series on American immigration and a series of four books on the Cold War. Michael has a bachelor of arts degree in history from the University of Connecticut and resides in that state.*